Copyright © 2025 by Educate Learners

Published by Educate Learners

All rights reserved. No part of this publication may be reproduced, distributed, or transmitted in any form or by any means, including photocopying, recording, or other electronic or mechanical methods, without the prior written permission of the publisher, except in the case of brief quotations embodied in critical reviews and certain other noncommercial uses permitted by copyright law.

First Printing, 2025.

ISBN: 978-1-951573-50-8

www.educatelearners.com

RED

Red

is a primary color.

There are different shades of red.

Apple

Fire Truck

Things that are
Red

Rose

Stop Sign

Yellow

Yellow

is a primary color.

There are different shades of yellow.

Banana

School Bus

Things that are
Yellow

Chick

Lemon

BLUE

Blue

is a primary color.

There are different shades of blue.

Blueberries

Jeans

Things that are
Blue

Blue Whale

Sky

ORANGE

Orange

is a secondary color.

Yellow

+

Red

=

Orange

There are different shades of orange.

Orange

Goldfish

Things that are
Orange

Basketball

Pumpkin

GREEN

Green

is a secondary color.

Yellow

+

Blue

=

Green

There are different shades of green.

Broccoli

Grasshopper

Things that are
Green

Grass

Grapes

PURPLE

Purple

is a secondary color.

Red

+

Blue

=

Purple

There are different shades of purple.

Amethyst

Grapes

Things that are
Purple

Eggplant

Lavender

BROWN

Brown

is a tertiary color.

Red

\+

Orange

=

Brown

There are different shades of brown.

Wood

Dirt

Things that are
Brown

Chocolate

Grizzly Bear

PINK

Pink

is a light red color.

Red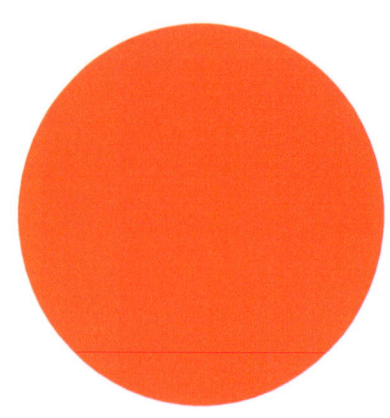

+

White

=

Pink

There are different shades of pink.

Pig

Flamingo

Things that are
Pink

Eraser

Bubblegum

GRAY

Gray

is a light black color.

Black

+

White

=

Gray

There are different shades of gray.

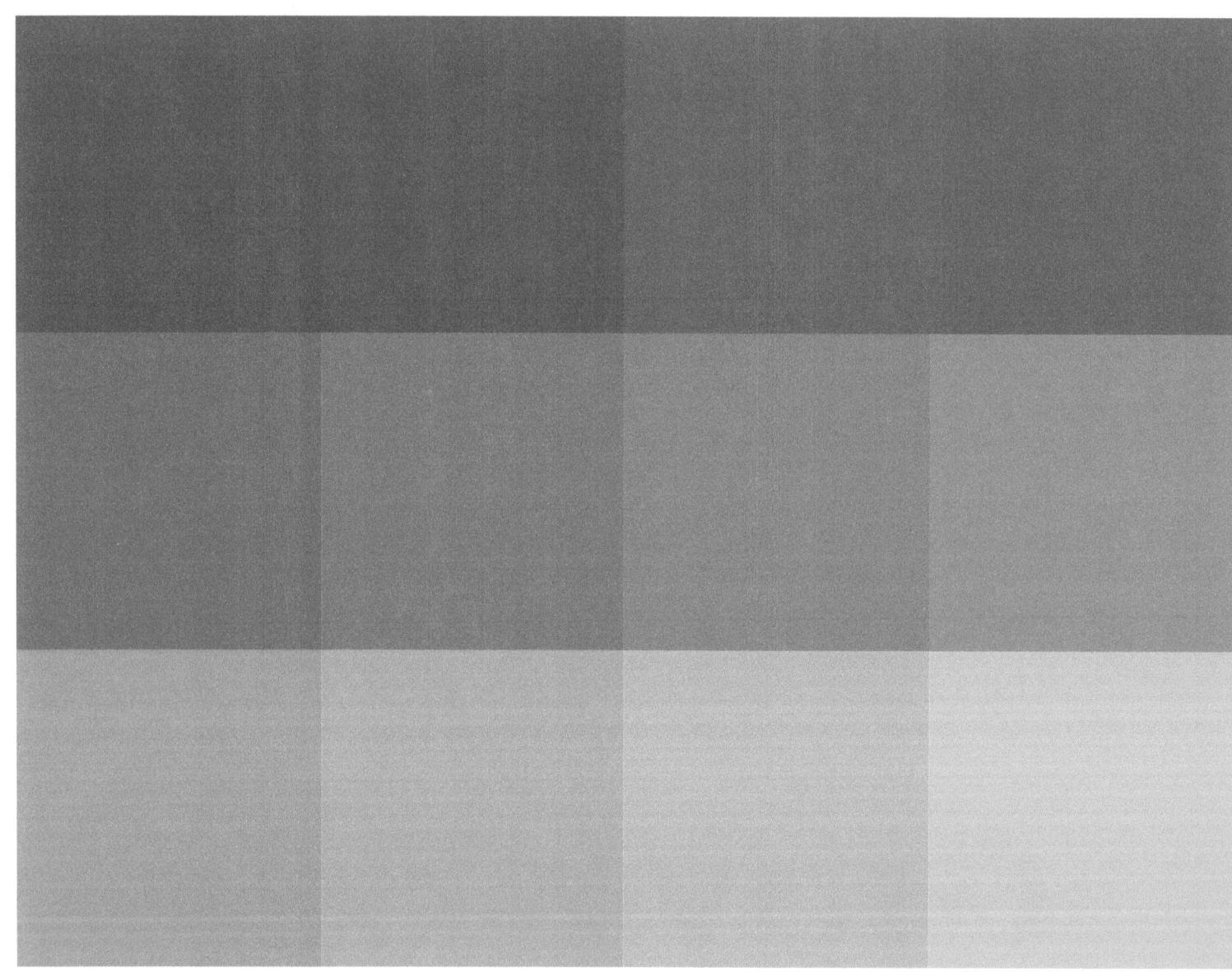

Koala

Rock

Things that are Gray

Rhinoceros

Elephant

BLACK

Black

is the darkest color.

There are different shades of **black**.

Crow

Ant

Things that are Black

Coal

Tire

WHITE

White

is the lightest color.

There are different shades of white.

Polar Bear

Cloud

Things that are White

Rice

Snowman

Thank you for reading!

Get a free year long subscription to our online education resource library when you purchase any one of our books.

Code: EDBOOKS

educatelearners.com

www.ingramcontent.com/pod-product-compliance
Lightning Source LLC
Chambersburg PA
CBHW041602070526
44586CB00003BA/48